LET'S GO TEAM:
Cheer, Dance, March

Competitive Cheerleading

Techniques of Dance for Cheerleading

History of Cheerleading

Techniques of Cheerleading

Chants, Cheers, and Jumps

Going to College

Dance Teams

Color Guard Competition

Techniques of Color Guard

Marching Band Competition

Techniques of Marching Bands

Cheerleading Stars

LET'S GO TEAM:
Cheer, Dance, March

Going to COLLEGE

Doris Valliant

Mason Crest Publishers
Philadelphia

Mason Crest Publishers, Inc.
370 Reed Road
Broomall, PA 19008
(866) MCP-BOOK (toll free)
www.masoncrest.com

First printing

1 2 3 4 5 6 7 8 9 10

Library of Congress Cataloging-in-Publication Data

Valliant, Doris.
  Going to college / Doris Valliant.
      p. cm. — (Let's go team — cheer, dance, march)
Includes bibliographical references and index.
  ISBN 1-59084-541-2
1. College choice — United States. 2. Cheerleading — United States.
3. Marching bands — United States. 4. Marching drills — United States.
5. Scholarships — United States. I. Title. II. Series.
  LB2350.5 .V35 2003
  378.1'942—dc21
                                  2002015961

Produced by
Choptank Syndicate and Chestnut Productions
226 South Washington Street
Easton, Maryland 21601

Project Editors Norman Macht and Mary Hull
Design Lisa Hochstein
Picture Research Mary Hull

Printed and bound in the Hashemite Kingdom of Jordan

OPPOSITE TITLE PAGE

More than 180 college cheerleading squads and dance teams traveled to Daytona Beach, Florida, to compete in the 2002 Chick-fil-A Cheer and Dance Collegiate Championships.

Table of Contents

Chapter 1
College Opportunities 7

Chapter 2
Cheerleading 15

Chapter 3
Dance and Drill Teams. 27

Chapter 4
Band and Guard. 39

Chapter 5
Scholarships and Benefits. 51

Glossary 60

Internet Resources 62

Further Reading 63

Index 64

College
Opportunities

Going to college is more than preparing for a future career. It's also a time to have fun and make life-long friends. At the college level, cheerleading, dance teams, color guard, and marching band involve exciting travel and performance opportunities with some of the most outstanding programs in the nation.

Joining a college marching band provides students an opportunity to play their instruments while becoming a member of a larger social circle. As you learn the band's marching style and formations, you also gain skill in working with others. Being able to work successfully with a diverse group of individuals is often a requirement in

A Purdue University trombonist cheers on the school's team during a football game. The Purdue All-American Marching Band is one of the best in the country and is open to students by audition.

today's workplace. A good way to gain this valuable experience is as a member of a dance team, cheerleading squad, color guard, or marching band.

Many university bands have illustrious pasts, and they continue to develop new marching innovations to match the ever-changing patterns of today's music. An important part of the marching band is the color guard. Color guards are often described as pageantry because these talented young adults provide an elaborate, grand display that is as entertaining as the intricate loops, scripts, and formations carried out by the marching band.

The Purdue University All-American Marching Band in West Lafayette, Indiana has a membership of nearly 400 students. Participation can earn two hours of academic credit. The band includes a full contingent of woodwinds, brass, and percussion instruments, the Golduster Dance/Drill Team, the All-American Flag Corps, the Twirling Corps, the Solo Twirlers, and the World's Largest Drum, the most visible symbol of any collegiate band in the nation.

College opportunities also abound for cheerleaders, dance teams, and pom squads. Like the marching band and color guard, these activities require a big time commitment. In fact, cheerleaders and dance teams may not miss a game. Most spirit squads attend summer practices and camps, rehearse over holiday breaks, and participate in national competitions.

Many cheerleading and dance team programs lack sufficient funding, so team members raise money as well as pay some expenses out of their own pockets.

There are many college-level opportunities for students interested in cheerleading or dance teams. In addition to providing support for their school teams, these groups often compete on their own.

Students who participate in groups like color guard, marching band, cheerleading, or dance teams build close friendships and develop teamwork skills that enrich their resumes.

Even though money is often an issue, many scholarships are available, especially in cheerleading, dance, and gymnastics. Scholarships for marching band and color guard are not as numerous, but they do exist. The best way to find scholarships is to talk with a school's financial aid department. The college admissions officer may be able to answer scholarship questions during a campus visit. Most colleges and universities have email addresses and/or Web sites that can provide a wealth of information about their particular programs and the scholarship opportunities available.

With so many colleges to choose from, the first step is to decide which one is for you. Make some selections, then research these schools and their programs on the Internet. Be sure to consider the costs of traveling to and from the college and your home. If you have to fly across the country every time you go home, you may not want to pick that particular school, especially if money is an issue. Consider the cost of living in that area; it may be more expensive to go to a university in a large metropolitan area like New York City than attend a college in a small town. However, a small town won't have all the opportunities that a city can offer.

The best way to decide, once you've researched schools and talked with your guidance counselor, is to travel to a school. On your visit, talk to admissions officers and take a tour of the campus and the facilities. Colleges and universities have student ambassadors who

HOW DO YOU
BEGIN A COLLEGE SEARCH?

Two useful college search tools are Peterson's and The College Board. Both have Web sites that are powerhouses of information.

Peterson's can be accessed at:
http://www.petersons.com.

The College Board is at:
http://www.collegeboard.org.

Peterson's and the College Board also have many publications that can help you decide where you want to go. Both publications and Web sites provide scholarship information.

will take you and your parents for a tour and answer your questions.

If you don't connect with the school and its campus and programs, then it may not be for you. No matter how great the cheerleading, dance team, or band programs may be, if you don't like the school and don't feel comfortable there, look elsewhere. There are many, many cheerleading, dance team, and band programs in universities large and small. Find the one that fits you and meets your needs.

Once you've narrowed your search, begin to investigate the cheerleading, dance team, or band programs. One reason you picked these schools was for their programs. Contact the coaches or advisors. Write a letter to these people or their departments, using your most professional voice and best writing skills. Ask them about

UNIVERSITY OF MARYLAND MASSED BAND DAY

Massed Band Day, one of the University of Maryland Marching Band traditions, occurs every year during the first home football game. High school bands from all over the mid-Atlantic region gather to march with the Maryland band during the halftime show. The 250-member Maryland Marching Band adds 2,500 to 3,000 students from Delaware, Maryland, Virginia, West Virginia, Pennsylvania, New York, and New Jersey to its Saturday performance. The high school bands rehearse with the Maryland band in the morning, and then participate in the halftime show's formations and music that afternoon.

scholarships and financial aid. Find out what expenses you will be expected to meet to be part of their program. The schools' Web sites may answer many of your questions, but be prepared to do additional research.

You may need videos and references for tryouts, so have these ready to go. Don't list any name as a reference unless you have personally asked that person to be a reference. You don't want any unpleasant surprises.

Be sure you meet any deadlines. You want to show the school that you are prepared and on time. Keep copies of everything you send out, and keep a record of the feedback you receive.

If you follow these steps, you will be ready to stunt, fly, high kick, twirl, march, or cheer your way through four years of academic learning. You'll improve your skills, make many new friends, and have fun.

Cheerleading

Cheerleading in college is different from cheerleading in high school. Although high school spirit leaders put in many after-school hours, college cheerleading often requires an even greater time commitment. Most college and university cheerleading squads are either all-girl, co-ed, or pom. A pom squad is another kind of pep squad. It always performs with pom pons, and is often a dance team as well. A cheerleading squad may also use pom pons in their routines, but not all the time.

Sometimes all three spirit groups boost fan enthusiasm during a single game, especially during football and men's basketball seasons. Although the primary goal of

The University of Kentucky cheerleaders have distinguished themselves at national cheerleading competitions and are 12-time winners of the UCA National College Championship.

college cheerleaders is to support the various university athletic programs, they also serve as important representatives of their university and often participate in various charitable and community events.

Some colleges, such as Northwestern University in Evanston, Illinois, consider cheerleading a sport. Others, like the University of Kentucky, consider cheerleading a student activity even though it's listed as part of the university's athletic Web site. Many college and university programs fall under the school's athletic department. Some are elite programs that draw students who hope to become part of these top-notch groups.

Pennsylvania State University has one of the top cheerleading programs in the nation. Candidates hoping to make either the co-ed or the all-girl team must display exceptional gymnastic skills and stunting abilities. Both men and women must complete the standing back tuck and standing handspring back tuck. Women need experience with co-ed and all-girl stunting, and men need some stunting experience.

Penn State's rival for the number one spot is the University of Kentucky (UK). The Kentucky cheerleading squad has won the UCA National College Cheerleading Championship for NCAA Division 1-A schools a remarkable 12 times. UK requires the same tucks as Penn State, but adds two other gymnastics skills. Stunting involves a toss shoulder stand, a toss heel-stretch, and one other stunt combination. UK candidates must make up their own cheer, which may include only two stunts and one gymnastics skill. Like most other collegiate tryouts, UK

The Pennsylvania State University cheerleaders are known for their gymnastic skills.

candidates must perform the school fight song with smiles, projection, and a sense of rhythm.

An interview is often part of the tryout process because universities want strong communication skills along with exceptional athletic talent. University of Kentucky judges evaluate candidates on their cheers, enthusiasm, and appearance in addition to their athletic abilities. During the interview, the coaches examine a candidate's ability to communicate, personality, and

Because cheerleaders represent their school at competitions and other events, they must exhibit enthusiasm, athleticism, poise, neatness, and goodwill.

attitude. Appearance is always an issue because coaches want cheerleaders who exhibit neatness, poise, and good posture.

Many universities have more than one squad. At Duke University in Durham, North Carolina, one of the NCAA powerhouses, the cheerleading squads are divided into the Blue and White squads. The Blue squad supports the men's basketball and football teams and holds tryouts after men's basketball season. Seniors, juniors, and second-semester sophomores can audition for the Blue squad.

Freshmen and beginning sophomores may try out for the White squad, which roots for women's basketball and the football teams. The Duke Web site says the cheerleading coaching staff looks for "potential rather than perfection" because they recognize the pressure and anxiety of auditioning.

The University of Kentucky Blue (Varsity) and White (Junior Varsity) squads are based on levels of cheerleading experience, and potential is a key element. Candidates trying out for the Blue squad already have noteworthy cheering experience along with poise, excellent athletic abilities, proper technical skills, and the ability to communicate. Even though they are scored on their "future potential" at tryouts, Blue squad members immediately

THE NCAA

The National Collegiate Athletic Association (NCAA), the governing body for all college athletic regulations and recruiting procedures, is made up of approximately 1,000 four-year colleges from large state universities to small private schools. The NCAA is divided into three divisions.

Division I schools are the biggest colleges and universities with the highest level of athletic competition. These schools award full and partial athletic scholarships.

Division II schools are smaller colleges and universities that are not as athletically competitive, but do offer athletic scholarships.

Division III schools are smaller colleges and universities that are less athletically competitive and offer no sports scholarships.

contribute to the cheerleading program because of their expertise.

The "future potential" score is especially important for White squad candidates because they are the feeder group to the Blue squad. White squad members are sophomores and incoming freshmen who have proper technical skills, athletic ability, communication skills, and poise. Although the White squad is not the most experienced, they demonstrate the potential to contribute to the program. Most important, they show promise to become future Blue squad members.

In addition to cheerleading skills, candidates must prove they are physically fit. At Duke, candidates do sit-ups and push-ups and run timed laps and sprints. At Howard University in Washington, D.C., candidates who make it through the preliminary rounds are immediately tested for fitness. Women must demonstrate the number of dips they can do, and men must show the number of times they can bench press their weight. College programs require their cheerleaders to have medical insurance and complete some kind of medical packet that involves a physical exam and medical history.

Many universities try to ease the anxiety of trying out for the cheerleading squad by holding clinics prior to the actual tryout date. The University of Kentucky holds three days of clinics during the tryout process to teach hopefuls new material as coaches evaluate partner stunting and gymnastic skills. Indiana University holds a Saturday clinic in February to sharpen cheering skills and prepare hopefuls for spring tryouts. The cost is only $25,

In addition to providing vocal support and enthusiasm for their school's sports teams, college cheerleaders represent their school at community events. Some squads also travel to compete in national cheerleading competitions.

and instructors are former Indiana cheerleaders and pom squad members.

At the University of Minnesota, cheerleaders give cheer and stunting clinics throughout the year for hopefuls who have never practiced co-ed cheering skills. Minnesota, where cheerleading got its start in 1898, has 28 to 40 co-ed positions available on its three spirit squads.

Not all tryouts are as stressful as those at the leading American universities. At Acadia University in Wolfville, Nova Scotia, Canada, cheerleading and gymnastics experience is not a prerequisite to be chosen for the squad. The Acadia coach looks for athletic ability. From January through April all students who want to be part of the cheerleading squad may take part; no one is cut. To cover the various sporting events, the coach divides the cheerleaders among the different events.

Cheerleaders not only support athletic teams, they also represent their schools in a variety of projects. The Harvard University cheerleaders serve as ambassadors to the greater Boston community, participating in the ArtsFirst Parade and Boston Bruins College Night. Penn State cheerleaders visit hospitals and retirement villages, work with the Nittany Lions Club, and participate in charitable fundraisers. The James Madison University cheerleaders in Virginia work with Special Olympics, March of Dimes, and United Way. The University of Louisville cheerleaders join student athletes in CardsCare, a community service project that enhances the interaction between the university and the community.

Louisville's Division 1-A cheerleading program has won national championships in co-ed, all-girl, and mascot competitions. However, like all cheerleading programs, academics are the first priority. Louisville cheerleaders must be full-time students who maintain at least a C (2.0) grade point average. Most collegiate cheerleaders are required to meet similar standards. Academic help offered to athletes is often available to cheerleaders.

Keeping the required academic grade point average is just one part of the large time commitment cheerleading demands. Penn State spirit squads know that from early August through the first week of April they must fulfill their responsibilities. This time commitment might even involve sacrificing fall, spring, and holiday breaks. When the rest of the Penn State student body is enjoying time off, the cheerleading squads have to cover any sports events scheduled during these breaks.

The University of Western Ontario Mustang Cheerleaders participate in the Orientation Week program, the Homecoming Parade, Alumni Department promotions, and other civic and corporate events in addition to their regular sports commitments and competition practices.

Cheerleaders may travel extensively, which is a valuable educational experience and another time commitment. The University of Kentucky squad has traveled to Canada, Mexico, Europe, Japan, and throughout the United States. Anyone who is not interested in traveling should not try out for the Kentucky team.

Regular practice sessions are always an obligation. Cheerleaders must attend scheduled two-hour practice sessions two or three times a week. In addition, cheerleaders are expected to work out several times a week to keep their bodies in peak condition. The Acadia University cheerleading team practices four times a week and lifts weights three times a week.

Many college cheerleading programs require their squads to attend training camps. The University of Western Ontario cheerleaders travel south to Louisville, Kentucky, for an NCA summer camp. Once they return to London, Ontario, they must participate in an intense three-day pre-season prep camp. The Indiana University cheerleaders must attend a weekend summer practice in June, the UCA/UDA summer camp in August, and a practice weekend before the regular fall academic session begins.

Indiana University advises their spirit groups, which include co-ed and all-girl cheerleading squads as well as an all-girl pom squad, that their personal expenses could run between $200 and $400, not including running shoes. In addition, each squad member is required to get two $500 program sponsorships or one $750 program sponsorship. These sponsorships help pay for camp expenses, uniforms, other cheer clothes, and expenses. Cheerleaders who fail to get the needed sponsorships are asked to pay all expenses usually covered by the cheerleading program. However, Indiana does not want to lose a quality candidate, so they offer to help find financial assistance for those individuals who cannot afford the costs of being a cheerleader.

To become a college cheerleader, you must first decide if you have the athletic ability and gymnastic skills needed to cheer at the college level. If you do, how much time are you willing to give to cheerleading? Are you academically strong enough to keep up your grades and attend all the practices and games required of the cheerleading squad? You may want to compete for a national title in addition to all the other cheerleader commitments. The last step is deciding which colleges and universities offer the programs that will best fit your skills and goals.

It's important to get college cheerleading coaches to notice you. One way to do this is to attend summer camp, since many cheerleading camps are held on college campuses. Often the staff are college cheerleaders and coaches. For example, the Universal Cheerleaders Association camps are staffed with some of the best college cheerleaders. College coaches often scout these camps looking for promising high school spirit leaders.

Another way to get the attention of college coaches is to send a videotape of yourself performing your best and most difficult skills, including a standing back tuck or a standing handspring back tuck. If you can do running tumbling, that's also a plus. If you are sending your tape to a co-ed squad, show your best stunts. If you want to be part of an all-girl squad, show just all-girl stunts.

Don't forget to let your personality shine in your videotape. Put on your best smile and have fun showing off your skills. Be sure to attach your name, return address, and phone number to the tape you send.

You may need to be persistent and call the coach rather than wait for the coach to call you. Remember, coaches receive many videotapes every day. Don't get lost in that pile of tapes. Let the coaches know you are truly interested in cheering for their school by calling them. However, once you've made contact, don't be a pest.

Another way to get noticed is simply to call the coach and ask for information about the cheerleading program. Or go to an open practice. Maybe they'll let you practice with them. You will also see how serious college cheering can be, which might help you decide if cheerleading in college is for you.

Don't be disappointed if you don't make the squad. Cheerleading in college is tough and highly competitive. You'll find many opportunities to show your spirit even if it's not in a cheerleader's uniform.

Dance and
Drill Teams

Dance and drill teams are a vital component of many college and university spirit squads. College opportunities for dance and drill teams run a close second to those for cheerleading. The DanceUSA.com Web site lists over 280 college and university dance, drill, and pom squads. These teams include two-year and four-year colleges and universities in Canada and the United States.

These college and university teams perform a variety of dance styles. Most use hip hop and jazz, but they also mix in funk, military, precision, kick and high kick, ballet, lyrical, swing, technical, character, novelty, street dance, color guard, and tap. Some, like those of

Using a medical theme that included nurse outfits and music like Madonna's "Fever," Harvard's Crimson dance team took fourth place at the 2002 NDA Collegiate Championship.

Mississippi State University and the University of Maryland Eastern Shore, are exclusively pom squads. Whether a pom squad or a dance/drill team, all require high-level technical skills and a willingness to adhere to rigorous practice and game schedules.

College level dance teams look for flexibility and skills such as splits, split leaps, kicks, high kicks, double and triple pirouettes, switch leaps, side leaps, and *fouettes,* dance steps that involve a whipping movement of the body. Toe touches can include a toe touch jump and tilted toe touch. Turns can involve double and triple turns, fouette turns, and pique and chaine turns, continuous turns on alternating feet.

Besides technical agility, members must maintain a C or better grade point average in four or more academic courses. In addition to technical and academic skills, coaches want their team members to practice healthy living and eating habits that allow them to meet the strenuous physical demands. Workouts involving muscle conditioning and aerobic training are also an essential part of a dance team's routine.

College dancing drill teams began in 1940 with the Kilgore Rangerettes of Kilgore College in Texas. The Rangerettes travel all over the world, and every year they perform at the New Year's Cotton Bowl Classic in Dallas, Texas. They were one of the first groups to appear at the inaugural parade for President George W. Bush. Over the years articles in major American magazines like *Sports Illustrated* and *Newsweek* have been written about the Rangerettes.

The Kilgore College Rangerettes were the first college drill team in the country. The Rangerettes travel extensively and perform at events like the Cotton Bowl.

A Rangerette carries a full course load plus rehearsals every afternoon. These rehearsals are part of her semester class schedule. Sometimes additional rehearsals are needed. Rangerettes must perform their distinctive high kick, but they also must maintain a C average or better while successfully completing 12 or more credit hours each semester. If a Rangerette's grade point average falls below the required standard, she faces performance suspension or dismissal from the squad. All Rangerettes must live on campus, and they stay in their own dormitory.

Once a dancer becomes a Kilgore Rangerette, she is forever a Rangerette. In 1979 former Rangerettes established a unique alumni group, Rangerettes Forever. Many of these former Rangerettes have not lost their abilities to kick high, and they sometimes perform with the current Kilgore Rangerettes.

Another world-famous college dance and drill team kicks their heels not far away from Kilgore College.

Since the 1950s the Tyler Junior College Apache Belles of Tyler, Texas have rivaled the Rangerettes. The Apache Belles have performed their high-stepping synchronized dance routines in many American cities and foreign countries, and for seven United States presidents. They have also performed at Disney World and they were a popular summer attraction at a Six Flags amusement park outside Dallas, Texas.

Not all collegiate dance and drill teams have the illustrious past and present of the Rangerettes and Apache Belles, but most demand the same kind of academic and technical excellence. Some teams want their members to maintain a grade point average higher than a C.

The Southeast Missouri State University Sundancers require a team grade point average of 3.0 or higher. This NCAA Division 1 university spirit squad is advised to study at least two hours outside of class for every hour they spend in class. That's in addition to practicing four days a week in the university's dance facilities and completing eight hours of weight lifting and aerobic workouts each week. The Sundancers want their team members to "dance, perform, sparkle, and enjoy the true team concept." However, the Sundancers remind their team members that they are "students first and dancers second."

At Sam Houston State University in Huntsville, Texas, members of the Orange Pride Dance Team can earn credit towards the physical education classes that are required of all SHSU students. University physical education courses are probably much less intense than any day of a dance team practice.

Most universities supply athletic trainers, workout facilities, uniforms, and traveling costs for the dance team. However, each dancer often has to pay for her tights, shoes, camp clothes, socks, and jackets. These costs usually run about $200 per dancer.

Some college programs also require team members to raise funds. At Towson University in Towson, Maryland,

GUSSIE NELL DAVIS

The concept of dance and drill teams began in 1929 when Miss Gussie Nell Davis started the first dancing pep squad at Greenville High School in Greenville, Texas. Ten years later the Dean at Kilgore College wanted a way to attract young women to the college and keep people entertained at football games during halftime. Miss Davis and her Greenville High School "Flaming Flashes" had gained recognition, and the Dean decided Kilgore College needed Miss Davis and her "show business" style concept for a college dancing drill team. In 1940, the Kilgore Rangerettes made their debut on the football field, and the dancing drill team was born.

During the 40 years that Gussie Nell Davis directed the Kilgore Rangerettes, the group traveled over a million miles as they represented the United States and Texas all over the globe. In 1975 the Houston Contemporary Museum of Art honored Miss Davis as a "living art form."

Miss Davis received many outstanding awards during her life, such as induction into the Texas Women's Hall of Fame and the Cotton Bowl Hall of Fame. This Texas legend died in 1993, but the techniques and traditions that Miss Davis began live on. The Rangerette dormitory at Kilgore College carries her name.

A dance team performs at the 2002 National Dance Alliance Collegiate Championship. In addition to participating in pep rallies and other school or community events, college dance teams attend camps and clinics to improve their skills, and they compete at dance competitions.

fundraising is a major component of their program. The Towson University Dance Team has been National Dance Alliance (NDA) champions. However, these champions still have to raise funds, using activities like stadium clean-ups, car washes, raffles, calendar sales, and advertisement distributions.

The York University Danz Team is a fairly new part of the spirit squad at York University in Toronto. Like their American counterparts, the Danz Team raises funds by selling chocolate bars at the school's football, basketball, and volleyball games as well as raffle tickets and York Danz Team t-shirts.

The York University Danz Team has 54 members, but most college dance teams are made up of 12 to 20 members. College dance teams participate in pep rallies, athletic events, and community events. Many dance team members also hold part-time jobs in addition to their academic classes. Members are warned that dance team must come ahead of job commitments. Work schedules should not conflict with practice, games, or other required events such as camps and competitions.

Most collegiate teams require members to attend a summer spirit camp, usually held by the Universal Dance Association (UDA), National Dance Alliance (NDA), or National Cheerleaders Association (NCA). Often dance team members must pay the cost of the camp. Dance team members usually return to school a week before the fall semester begins to practice and get routines ready for the upcoming athletic seasons. Many teams also compete in UDA and/or NDA National Championships, which means additional time commitments for practice and travel, as well as additional expense.

Many of these competitions are held in Orlando or Daytona Beach, Florida, and some occur early in January. For dance team members, this means after they complete final exams and go home for a short winter break, they must return to school right after New Year's to prepare for national competition.

Some teams compete internationally. The George Brown College Dance Team of Toronto traveled to

Germany to participate in the World Cheer and Dance Championships.

The St. John's University Red Storm Dance Team, which has been in existence for over 40 years at the Jamaica, New York school, performs at all home football and basketball games. Basketball games include dancing on the center court in front of 19,000 excited fans at one of the most famous sports arenas in the world, Madison Square Garden in New York City. Because St. John's

JUGGLING DANCE CLASS AND DANCE TEAM

Dance team members need to keep their jazz and ballet skills sharp. How do they manage all the practice hours dance team requires and still find time to attend dance classes? Usually dancers have to make choices, and they must tell their dance teachers that they are also part of a school dance team. They need to have realistic expectations. Dance team members may not be able to dance the lead role in a ballet because they already have a big time commitment on the dance team.

Whether dancing on a team or in a dance class, dancers must begin with warm-up and stretching routines to avoid injuries. Dancers trying to juggle both class and team must not make the mistake of not taking time to warm up. Failure to warm up means increasing opportunities for injuries that could sideline a dancer's career.

Dancers must also wear the proper shoes when they are doing their dance team routines, usually athletic shoes with firm support or jazz shoes, always keeping in mind the type of routine, the level of impact, and the kind of surface they're dancing on.

The ability to do high kicks is important for all dancers, and especially for drill team members, as a kickline is often a major component of their performance.

University is so close to New York City, many of the team members also attend classes at famous New York dance studios.

Some college dance team programs also sponsor youth programs. The Southeast Missouri State University Sundancers hold "Sunbeam Clinics" for girls and boys ages 3 to 12. In 2002 George Mason University in Fairfax, Virginia started Junior Masonettes. These young dancers in grades three to eight attended one or two dance clinics to learn the Masonettes dance routines. Not long after the clinics were held, the Junior Masonettes joined the Masonettes Dance Team and showed off their new skills in pre-game and halftime performances at George Mason University's men's and women's basketball games.

To accentuate their arm movements and add visual interest, dance teams sometimes incorporate pom pons as part of their routines. A dance team that always performs with pom pons, however, is known as a pom squad.

Dance teams are highly visible representatives of their colleges and universities. In their dazzling costumes and bright makeup, the dancers serve as ambassadors for the school. Whether dance team members are in uniform or out of uniform, the image they project reflects on the athletic teams they support and on their school.

College dance team standards are rigorous. Mandatory practices and events demand a big time commitment from all dancers. Team members must also successfully complete their academic courses and maintain the team's required grade point average.

A dance team is a group of individuals who must work closely together to attain a goal, which for this particular kind of team means a synchronized, carefully choreographed routine and drill. To succeed at the college level takes perseverance and a dedication to quality. The teamwork and discipline required to be part of this effort prepare dance team members for later career success. Dance team members graduate from college and go on to successful professional careers in medicine, business, education, law, and many other fields.

Band and Guard

 ollege students don't have to be music majors to participate in the marching band. Only about a quarter of the membership in marching bands are music majors; the rest are students majoring in a variety of academic subjects. At many universities the marching band students maintain higher grade point averages than the rest of the student body and participate in many other campus activities. Many marching band students are in honors programs, the most academically rigorous courses on campus. These enthusiastic students choose marching band to play their instruments or twirl their batons, sabers, rifles, and flags. College marching bands are an

Like all marching band members, the color guard must practice frequently. Some guard members enter indoor winter guard competitions after the marching band season ends.

exciting way to build friendships and create lifetime memories.

College marching bands range in size from less than 50 members to over 350 men and women. Many colleges are looking for bodies, not musicians. Marching Band Director Dr. L. Richmond Sparks of the University of Maryland wants numbers, so he'll take just about anyone who shows up to band camp. On the other hand, competition is stiff at Ohio State University. Even returning band members have to try out every year, and they may lose their spots to a newcomer, especially if the veteran has slacked off over the summer. Ohio State offers summer sessions for veterans and prospective band members who want to stay in shape for the upcoming season and practice the band's marching style and maneuvers.

Marching band is not a sport, but the Ohio State's Marching Band Web site makes it sound like one. It suggests that band members build up endurance for the fall marching season by running every day, including running up steps. They should also do basic sit-ups, push-ups, and stretch so that no one will pull a muscle a few days before tryouts.

To improve their marching skills band members are told, "Constantly work on your Eight to Five step. If that means marching up and down the field 20 times . . . do it!" After drilling the Eight to Five, or taking eight steps to march five yards, band members should stand in front of a full-length mirror and march in place, studying themselves and correcting any problems they see. Standing in front of a mirror, band members see how a maneuver should look and feel. Even better, band members should have someone videotape them marching.

If they cannot attend any summer sessions, prospective Ohio State band members are told to march at their high school field, or to drill up and down their back yards if they have nowhere else to march. "You may feel awkward," the band says, "but remember what you are trying out for!"

The Ohio State University Marching Band is one of the elite college bands in the country. It began in 1878 as a 12-piece fife and drum corps. The modern 225-member band is the largest all-brass and percussion band in the nation and a winner of the prestigious Sudler Trophy, given each year by the John Philip Sousa Foundation to the country's outstanding collegiate marching band.

Many modern marching band traditions, such as floating and animated formations, measured step marching, script writing, and the fast cadence with a high knee lift, were first developed at Ohio State. In 1920 OSU introduced Edwin "Tubby" Essington, the first collegiate strutting drum major. It is not surprising that competition is strong for positions on this prestigious band.

The Band of the Fighting Irish of the University of Notre Dame claims to be one of the oldest university bands in continual existence. Begun in 1845, the band has played for every home football game since 1887. It was among the first bands in the nation to use precision drill, pageantry, and picture formations. In 1976 the National Music Council named the Band of the Fighting Irish a "landmark of American Music." Today the Fighting Irish Band has about 340 members, representing every academic major on campus. It has performed at the Cotton Bowl, Sugar Bowl, Orange Bowl, Fiesta Bowl, and Gator Bowl.

The Cal Band of the University of California at Berkeley also has an illustrious past. The marching band began in 1889 as a Cadet Band, part of the Reserve Officers Training Corps (ROTC) program. In 1923 the ROTC Cadet Band became the University of California Marching Band. The modern 180-member band, known for its unique high-stepping marching style, is student-managed. Unlike many bands supported by the university music or athletic departments, the band must raise funds to meet over half of its budget.

What does it take to become a member of a college marching band? At Indiana University the Marching Hundred looks for basic rhythm, technical facility, and marching experience. Being a music major is not a requirement, but the Marching Hundred wants 300 men and women moving with snap and precision across the football field. A leader in drill design, the Marching Hundred entertains its audience with the highest quality floating letter formations, script writing, fast cadence, circle drills, and other marching innovations.

Prospective members learn all these maneuvers at band camp, which is held on campus usually a week or two before the fall semester starts. At Indiana University, prospective and veteran band members audition, then learn the drills and music. Band camp concludes with a

The Cal Band of the University of California at Berkeley is known for its high-stepping show band style.

special program called "An Evening at the House," when new and old band members march in Mellencamp Pavilion, find band stadium seats, and participate in an annual section competition.

At the University of Maryland, College Park, band members report for Early Week a week before students return to campus. Amanda Brown, a Maryland marching band member from the class of 2003, describes a typical day during Early Week:

Breakfast is at 7 A.M. At 7:30 you have to be on the field. Then we rehearse from 7:30 till 10:30. Eleven o'clock is

Being part of a college or university marching band is a huge time commitment, but band members enjoy the comradery and often develop lifelong friendships.

lunch. We go inside for the heat of the day. From one till four we have sectionals and rehearsals and learn our music. Then we go back outside from 6 to 9 P.M. We have meetings at 9:30 with Dr. Sparks, our conductor, or others.

The day that began around 7 ends that night at 11. Brown points out, "If you can make it through Early

Week, you can make it through the season." This assessment probably holds true for collegiate marching band camps nationwide. In addition to the long days and endless drills and rehearsals, Early Week occurs in late August, which often means practicing in heat and humidity. Fortunately, band members are wearing shorts and t-shirts, not their heavy uniforms. When football season starts, the temperature is likely to match some of July's hottest days, but the band marches into the stadium and performs in full uniform.

While football season requires a full marching band to perform spectacular halftime shows, most colleges and universities use smaller pep bands of 125 members or less for men's and women's basketball games and other sports. Pep band is mostly brass and drum ensemble that is often made up of non-music majors. Like marching band, students in the pep band receive one to two college credits for each semester they participate.

According to Brown, there are "lots of perks" to being in a marching or pep band. At the 2002 NCAA Men's Basketball Championship game, the Maryland Pep Band was selected to play for the opening ceremony. Brown found herself tootling her baritone with tears running down her face as the Pep Band played "The Star-Spangled Banner" while the World Trade Center flag was carried in front of her and then presented to the officials. That spring she met President George W. Bush when the Pep Band played the music for a White House reception honoring NCAA championship winners from several different sports.

Marching band is a major time commitment that can become more difficult each year as students juggle academic classes, maintain grade point averages to hold onto academic and university scholarships, and work part-time jobs. At the University of Maryland about half of the band members are freshmen. These newcomers replace upper-classmen who can no longer manage the grueling schedule. From late August through Thanksgiving, most college bands rehearse six to ten hours a week in addition to the time involved at football games. Most marching bands start game days with a three-hour morning rehearsal before stepping off for pre-game, halftime, and post-game shows.

Not every marching band performer plays an instrument. Some members twirl batons. Others execute seemingly impossible leaps and turns using colorful flags, silver sabers, wooden rifles, and an assortment of other props as members of the color guard section.

For example, the Indiana Marching Hundred Flag Corps is an elite group of 24 experienced flag corps performers, who must audition on the first day of band camp. The Marching Hundred also includes the RedSteppers, a dance line of highly talented women who perform special routines with the band during each pre-game, halftime, and post-game show. Like the Flag Corps, the RedSteppers are experienced dancers who must audition in the spring or fall during band camp.

At the University of Maryland, the color guard/flag section of the marching band is called the Silks. The Silks, who include baton twirlers, practice every day because their routines take lots of coordination. While the Silks are practicing every day, the marching band drills five out of seven days during football season. Everyone shows up at 8 A.M. on game days for the three-hour rehearsal, followed by lunch. Then it's show time.

The Golden Delight flag and majorette squad of North Carolina A & T University adds precise twirling and energetic dancing to the nationally ranked Blue & Gold Marching Machine band. The Blue & Gold Marching Machine belongs to the "Sizzlin' Seven," an elite list of the best black college bands, which includes Southern University, Florida A & M, South Carolina State, Prairie View A & M, Jackson State, and Tennessee State.

MARCHING BANDS ARE AGELESS

Larry Schwab, a 61-year-old ophthalmologist from Morgantown, West Virginia, proves that you are never too old to march in the band. When the 339-member Pride of West Virginia University Marching Band walks onto the football field, it includes a baton twirler and this gray-haired doctor. Schwab last marched with the band as an undergraduate beginning in 1958. In 2001, Schwab decided it was time to give in to his long-held desire to march again and play his baritone horn. He enrolled in a one-credit university music class so that he could become a member of the WVU Mountaineer Band.

He continues to run an eye clinic in Morgantown while practicing 20 hours a week with the band. When football season ends, Schwab and his baritone join the pep band for basketball season.

The University of Maryland Marching Band performs with high school marching bands from the mid-Atlantic region during halftime at Massed Band Day, a University of Maryland tradition that takes place each year during the first home football game.

Maintaining this high ranking requires hard work and dedication. Band camp runs over two weeks for the Golden Delight and band members. All Golden Delight and band candidates must bring gold t-shirts, navy blue shorts, white athletic socks, Vaseline or muscle ointment for sore feet, and black leather military combat boots to band camp. Delights must also include sneakers appropriate for dancing, and show makeup. Band members need snacks to eat or drink before the 5 A.M. practice.

Many color guards continue to practice after the season ends, preparing to compete in Winter Guard International indoor competitions against hundreds of other color guards. The Riverside Community College of Riverside, California, has the Fantasia Winter Guard, who were 2000 and 2002 Winter Guard International Independent World Gold Medalists. They combine a diversity of flags, rifles, silks, even umbrellas and balloons, with jazz, pop, and modern dance, plus a touch of ballet.

The Ohio State University Marching Band Web site points out that trying out for any kind of marching unit is "not an impossible task." The Web site tells prospective band members to practice one maneuver at a time, breaking it into parts. If they follow this same procedure for the next maneuver, in time they will learn all they need to know. "Never say you're not good enough," OSU advises. These words could be spoken by college bandmasters everywhere.

The drills are tough, and the time commitment is even more difficult, but the discipline and work ethic band members develop become life-long skills that carry over into their future professional lives. The pride that comes from playing a band instrument, high-stepping down the street, falling into formation across the football field, or twirling a flag or baton is worth every moment.

Scholarships and Benefits

One way to help pay for college is to apply for scholarships. Scholarships are monies that do not have to be repaid, unlike the many kinds of college loans that require repayment over the years. Many cheerleading and dance team scholarships are available. Marching band and color guard scholarship opportunities are not as plentiful. The best way to find out about a particular kind of scholarship is to ask the admissions officer or talk with the band director, or cheerleading or dance team coach.

Cheerleading scholarships are not large sums of money, but they do help decrease the high cost of a college education. *American Cheerleader*, the leading

Some schools offer full tuition for varsity cheerleaders. Others offer smaller amounts, or they may assist cheerleaders by offering early registration for classes and covering the cost of textbooks, travel, and uniforms.

cheerleading magazine, details over 220 colleges that offer full and partial scholarships. Most cheerleading scholarships range between $500 and $600 a semester, or $1,000 to $1,200 a year. The University of Delaware offers one of the highest scholarship amounts. The top 12 cheerleaders, whom the University of Delaware Web site calls athletes, receive $4,000 a year in scholarships. Delaware requires the highest levels of tumbling and stunting skills, as well as exceptional cheerleading skills. In 2000–2001, the Delaware Blue Hen cheerleaders won

ALUMNI GROUPS KEEP THE SPIRIT

One benefit of being part of a spirit group is that many of these groups have alumni organizations. Alumni are graduates of a particular college or university. Marching bands have particularly active alumni groups. In fact, many colleges hold alumni reunions every season, giving graduates an opportunity to perform once again.

At Ohio State the Alumni Band reunions have produced a variation on the famous marching band formation called "Script Ohio," using four units to form the word "Ohio." This quadruple Script Ohio unites the present and past OSU bands. It is a tribute to a tradition that began at Ohio State in 1936 when the marching band first spelled out the word "Ohio" in cursive or script writing.

The Kilgore Rangerettes sometimes perform with their alumni organization, Rangerettes Forever. In the 1989 Macy's Thanksgiving Day Parade, the first captain of the Rangerettes, Judy Lyle Hale, led the Rangerettes Forever down the parade route. It was Hale's 65th birthday.

the Division 1 Nationals at the UCA National College Cheerleading Championships.

Besides scholarship money, cheerleaders often get to register early for classes. Since many classes fill up fast, early registration gives cheerleaders a better chance to get the classes they want. Some colleges and universities also pay for cheerleaders' books, which often can run over $500 a semester. At Middle Tennessee State University, members of the Blue squad, who cheer for football and men's basketball, are eligible to rent their books through the university bookstore. The cheerleading program will pay for books they can't rent if there is money in the cheerleading budget.

The Middle Tennessee State program, like most collegiate cheerleading programs, emphasizes academics as a first priority for cheerleaders. Many scholarships are based on grade point average, usually requiring a 2.0–2.5, which is in the C range.

At the University of Kentucky, Blue squad members receive scholarships that equal the amount of in-state tuition. Students whose homes are outside Kentucky are given a portion of their out-of-state tuition fees. For those UK cheerleaders on both the Blue and White squads with a GPA of at least 3.0 (a B), additional scholarship money is awarded.

Penn State University gives a $1,500 scholarship for cheerleaders who maintain a 3.0 cumulative GPA. The University of Louisville awards scholarships at the end of tryouts to the top 10 men and top 10 women based on their financial need, skills, and grades. If Louisville

Dancers and cheerleaders can compete for scholarships in Dallas, Texas, at the National Best Cheerleader and Dancer Scholarship Championship held by the National Spirit Group. Competition categories include individual cheer and dance, group stunt, partner stunt, and mascot.

cheerleaders keep their GPA on the high end after the fall semester, the scholarships carry over to the spring semester. Falling grades reduce scholarship amounts and can result in a loss of the scholarship entirely, which is true for other universities as well.

At the University of Mississippi, in addition to a $1,000-a-year scholarship for all cheerleading squads, Ole Miss pays all cheerleading expenses, including summer camp fees. When cheerleaders travel to away games, they are given $30 per day for expenses. Cheerleading also earns each member of the squad one academic credit, which usually means an A grade. If a cheerleader cheers for the four years at the university, this A gets added in with the other grades, which helps improve a cumulative GPA.

High grades are usually an entrance requirement for an Ivy League school like Harvard University. No Ivy League school gives any kind of scholarships—athletic or merit based. However, lack of funds shouldn't stop anyone from applying because Harvard has one of the best need-based financial aid systems in the country.

Financial aid at a non-Ivy League school can be a combination of scholarships and loans in the amount you need to pay your tuition, room, and board. Books, travel costs, and personal expenses are not part of the financial aid package; that's money you have to find.

Methodist College in Fayetteville, North Carolina, one of the top small college cheerleading programs in the country, bases scholarships on maintaining skills. Collegiate appearance and strong crowd appeal are very important, and cheerleaders must sustain their back hand-springs and strong motion techniques. They must keep their basic co-ed or advanced all-girl partner stunting techniques in top shape. Dance team members must have a strong toe touch, a switch leap, a double turn, an axel,

Winter Guard International is a source of scholarships for color guard and indoor percussion enthusiasts. The organization gives away over $20,000 each year to students who have been nominated by their unit and have participated in the WGI World Championships.

and a sharp motion technique. This Division II school has gained national championship rankings for its cheerleaders and dance team.

Dance team scholarships rank close to cheerleading scholarships in availability and amount. For instance, the scholarships for the Tyler Junior College Apache Belles dance/drill team members are performance grants of $300–$500 a semester. Drill team officers also get additional amounts.

Many dance team scholarships are based on length of time on the team. For example, at St. John's University second year Red Storm Dance Team members receive $1,000, third year get $1,500, and fourth year members get $2,000.

The Middle Tennessee University Lightning Dance Team scholarship program reflects the scale that many colleges and universities use. First years get $100 a semester, second years $200, third years jump to $400, and fourth years to $500 a semester. All MTSU Lightning Team members receive tuition and books each semester, regardless of their position on the team.

Marching band scholarships vary. The best way to determine if a band program offers scholarships is to contact the band director or the music department of the college or university, or check the school's Web site. Scholarships may be given to freshmen only or upper-classmen (juniors and seniors) only or to any band member. For example, at Brigham Young University in Utah, band members receive talent/service awards beginning at $300. The amount increases based on a band member's experience, leadership responsibilities, and instrumentation needs.

The Revelli Foundation, a non-profit charitable foundation dedicated to supporting music education through band, annually awards several scholarships to high school seniors who plan to pursue a career in music education. High school band directors nominate senior marching band members who plan to major in music education. These scholarships are presented at the National Concert Band Festival.

Winter Guard International (WGI) awards over $20,000 in scholarships, given in amounts of at least $500 each, to young performers who have been nominated by their Winter Guard unit participating in the World

Championships. The unit's nominee can be a high school senior or already enrolled in college. Nominees must have shown personal achievement and have outstanding academic and artistic qualities.

Many alumni groups are sources of scholarships for bands, cheerleading, and dance teams. For example, the Florida A & M University Marching "100" Alumni Band Association sponsors band camp scholarships. Because of the fundraising efforts of the Rangerettes Forever alumni group, every Kilgore College Rangerette receives a partial scholarship each semester. Other Rangerette scholarships are available based on scholastic averages and dance performance.

Several of the cheerleading and dance associations give scholarships to outstanding individuals. The World Cheerleading Association (WCA) gives $25,000 in scholarships to outstanding cheerleaders and dance members each year, and a $2,000 scholarship to the Cheerleader of the Year, who is selected at the WCA Nationals in Nashville, Tennessee. The National Spirit Group (NSG) annually sponsors the Annual Best Cheerleader and Dancer Scholarship Championship, which offers $30,000 in scholarships and prizes. Since 1988, Cheerleaders of America (COA) has awarded over $385,000 in scholarships to individuals and teams. In Canada, the Ontario Cheerleading Federation gives at least one $500 scholarship at the Ontario Cheerleading Championships final awards ceremony.

Some dance teams and cheerleading squads have created sponsor organizations to assist with the cost of uniforms, operations, and attending national competitions. Donations from friends, families, and corporate sponsors who make up the Friends of York Danz Team help decrease the personal costs to each member of the team. In 1997, the Friends of Harvard Cheerleading was established. Like the Friends of York Danz Team, the Friends of Harvard have aided Harvard cheerleaders so they can afford the high costs of cheerleading and still pay their other college expenses.

The scholarship money may not be large, but the benefits of cheerleading or participating in color guard, marching band, or dance team are enormous. For many college students this is their first time away from home. Being part of the band, color guard, dance team, or cheerleading squad creates a social structure and a kind of family support system. Whether the campus is small or has a huge student population, these spirit groups guide individuals into becoming mature and responsible adults who can live and work within a group. Spirit groups help their members develop teamwork skills that are essential in today's rapidly changing world.

Besides developing the academic and career skills so vital today, these spirit groups are fun. Cheerleading squads, dance teams, and the members of the marching bands often form bonds that last a lifetime. The performances, competitions, and travel opportunities provide their participants with enough memorable experiences to fill a football stadium.

Glossary

alma mater – The college or school a student attended; or, another name for the official school song.

ballet – A classical style of dance in which conventional poses and steps are combined with light, flowing leaps and turns.

choreography – The planning of the movements and steps of a dance routine.

color guard – A unit of a marching band that uses flags, rifles, sabers, and other props as part of a dance routine.

corps style – A style of marching that involves band members taking 8 steps to march 5 yards.

cumulative grade point average – The average of all the grades a student has earned for all courses taken.

fouette – A dance step that involves a whipping movement of the body.

funk – A style of dance that incorporates natural movements rather than arranged ones. Funk also incorporates street dances performed in American cities.

hip hop – A style of music and dance including rap and other contemporary upbeat music that is fast-paced and energetic. Dance movements are sharp, using break dancing and body popping gestures.

jazz – Dance movements that involve a variety of routines and are performed to jazz music or blues-style music. Jazz incorporates rhythms and techniques that isolate a particular part of the body in motion.

kick – A routine that uses kick sequences. Some kicks are waist high, others are head high.

lyrical – A form of modern dance that incorporates jazz and ballet movements with leaps, turns, and footwork.

military marching style – A regimental marching style with symmetrical formations marching and countermarching in long-striding 6 to 5 style, 6 steps to march 5 yards.

military and precision dance – Styles of dance that are much alike, using sharp arm, head, and leg movements. These routines look like military-style marching and they use precision visual formations, such as those performed by drill teams.

novelty – A dance routine formed around a theme, such as a character, concept, or particular song. Costumes and props are often part of novelty routines.

pageantry – Term used to describe the color guard, flag team, baton twirlers, or dance team that are often sections of the marching band.

pique and chaine turn – In classical ballet, a series of continuous turns on alternating feet with the body rotating rapidly.

pirouette – A turn or series of turns on one leg.

prerequisite – A requirement that must be fulfilled before something else can happen or be done.

swing – Dance performed to music that may be from rock, rhythm and blues, or the big band sound of the 1930s and 40s. Swing includes movements from such popular dances as the jitterbug and Charleston.

tap – A style of dance utilizing tap shoes, which produce a tapping sound when dancers move their feet in rhythmic patterns and movements.

Internet Resources

http://www.collegeboard.com/paying

The official site of the College Board offers expert advice on getting to college, as well as information about scholarships and interactive tools that can help you find financial aid.

http://www.gocollege.com

GoCollege.com offers information on colleges and universities and gives you tips on how to study for the SAT and ACT tests. This Web site also maintains a scholarship database that provides information on where to look for financial aid.

http://www.marching.com

Marching.com offers information on marching bands, including events and scores, resources, and links to other Web sites.

http://www.mddtusa.com

Miss Dance Drill Team USA is a non-profit organization dedicated to the advancement of students through the pep arts.

http://www.nationalspirit.com

The National Dance Alliance (NDA) and the National Cheerleading Association (NCA) are part of the National Spirit Group, a company offering summer camps, competitions, special events, and uniforms.

http://www.varsity.com

Offering information and resources for both cheerleading and dance, Varsity.com is home to the Universal Dance Association (UDA) and the Universal Cheerleaders Association (UCA).

http://www.wgi.org

Winter Guard International (WGI) sponsors regional marching band competitions as well as U.S. and Canadian contests for color guard and indoor percussion.

Further Reading

Garty, Judy. *Marching Band Competition.* Philadelphia, Pennsylvania: Mason Crest Publishers, 2003.

Garty, Judy. *Techniques of Marching Bands.* Philadelphia, Pennsylvania: Mason Crest Publishers, 2003.

Holston, Kim R. *The Marching Band Handbook.* Jefferson, North Carolina: McFarland & Company, 1994.

Neil, Randy, and Elaine Hart. *The Official Cheerleader's Handbook.* New York: Simon & Schuster, 1986.

Peters, Craig. *Cheerleading Stars.* Philadelphia, Pennsylvania: Mason Crest Publishers, 2003.

Peters, Craig. *Competitive Cheerleading.* Philadelphia, Pennsylvania: Mason Crest Publishers, 2003.

Scott, Kieran. *Ultimate Cheerleading.* New York: Scholastic, Inc., 1998.

Sloan, Karyn. *Techniques of Color Guard.* Philadelphia, Pennsylvania: Mason Crest Publishers, 2003.

Usilton, Terry. *Color Guard Competition.* Philadelphia, Pennsylvania: Mason Crest Publishers, 2003.

Valliant, Doris. *Dance Teams.* Philadelphia, Pennsylvania: Mason Crest Publishers, 2003.

Index

Acadia University cheerleaders, 21, 22, 23
Brigham Young University, 57
Davis, Gussie Nell, 31
Duke University cheerleaders, 18, 19, 20
Florida A & M University, 47, 58
George Brown College Dance Team, 34
George Mason University Masonettes Dance Team, 35
Harvard University, 22, 55, 59
Howard University cheerleaders, 20
Indiana University, 20, 21, 23, 24, 42, 43, 46
Jackson State University, 47
James Madison University cheerleaders, 22
Kilgore College Rangerettes, 28, 29, 31, 52, 58
Methodist College, 55
Middle Tennessee State University, 53, 57

Mississippi State University, 28
North Carolina A & T University Golden Delight, 47, 48
Northwestern University cheerleading, 16
Ohio State University Marching Band, 40, 41, 49, 52
Pennsylvania State University cheerleaders, 16, 22, 23, 53
Prairie View A & M, 47
Purdue University, 8
Riverside Community College Fantasia Winter Guard, 49
Sam Houston State University Orange Pride Dance Team, 30
South Carolina State, 47
Southeast Missouri State University Sundancers, 30, 35
Southern University, 47
St. John's University Red Storm Dance Team, 34, 35, 56
Tennessee State University, 47
Towson University Dance Team, 32

Tyler Junior College Apache Belles, 30, 56
University of California at Berkeley Cal Band, 42
University of Delaware, 52
University of Kentucky cheerleaders, 16–20, 23, 53
University of Louisville cheerleaders, 22, 53, 54
University of Maryland Eastern Shore pom squad, 28
University of Maryland Marching Band, 12, 40, 43–46, 47
University of Minnesota cheerleaders, 21
University of Mississippi, 55
University of Notre Dame Band of the Fighting Irish, 41, 42
University of Western Ontario Mustang cheerleaders, 23
West Virginia University Marching Band, 47
York University Danz Team, 32, 33, 59

DORIS VALLIANT teaches English at Easton High School in Easton, Maryland. She writes books for young people and articles for regional publications. She wasn't a cheerleader in high school, but two of her best friends were. She shouted with them at the Friday night football games and performed a skit or two at pep rallies.